This Book Belongs To:

_____

Attention Golden Bears,

There's something else to see...
Can you find the hidden paw print
on pages A through Z?

Special thanks to the Upper Arlington Education Foundation, Upper Arlington Schools, Melanie Brown, Dr. Katie Brownfield, Alice Finley, Missy Haines, Megan Potts, Colleen Wright, Jason Wulf, Kim Petersen, and the many students, staff members, and community members who offered their time and support.

The *Golden Bears A to Z* book format was inspired by the book *Buckeyes A to Z* by Mark Walter.

The *Golden Bears A to Z* Team

Staff Members: Blair Cerny, Jana Holland, Blythe Lamont, Jill Merkle, Jamie Trainor, and Mark Walter

Student Writing and Research Team: Yasin Sayed Ahmed, Iris Bachey, Elizabeth Bicknell, Hudson Copeland, Caroline Crespo, Addy Day, Hudson Davis, Lina Dendeni, Riley DuPont, Jack Elliott, Grace Garish, Aubrie Gorsline, Edie Hampel, Ian Hawley, Marie Hawley, Kristen Kahle, Sunny Li, Elise Lowe, Faith Markoff, Isaac Meats, Rourke Montgomery, Ben Obergefell, Joonyoung Park, Holly Piccin, Laiken Ramsey, Claire Shen, Alexi Shields, Sophia Spears, Jackson Stiles, Tamara Stone, Olivia Stuecher, Ella Tang, Penelope Thrush, Kaelin Valerio, Hailey Welch, and Lin Lin Xu

Student Editing Team: Catie Buffer, Mackenzie Enlow, Kevin Feng, Anna Cui, James Hawley, Emma Kowalski, Cameron Krisiewicz, Kiran Levacy-Baichu, Nancy Li, Emily Liu, Avery Lloyd, Jack Mandel, Hannah Nagase, Blaise Petersen, Ben Prescott, Marco Schoenherr, Carter Sisson, Jacob Stross, Ellen Wen, Thomas Wu, and Suri Zhu

Student Sales and Marketing Team: Hudson Belair, Paxton Endress, Sivan Freud, Madison Hanosek, Sydney Hart, Drew Hays, Cole Heublein, Beatrice Keenan, Yusef Khamis, Daphne Lanctot, Sarah McAllister, Paige McCandless, Beckett Montgomery, David Mousa, David Narcelles, Ella Oakes, Anthony Orr, Brennan Oswald, Caroline Overmyer, Tessa Pacanovsky, Mahaela Park, John Poole, Charlotte Potts, Ryan Potts, Jack Pruchnicki, Deven Reddy, Claire Richey, Max Rigrish, Audrey Sauk, Colin Short, Ryley Schneider, Elliot Stamm, Wagner Suh, Walter Thurston, Ishaan Vasudeva, and Katya Volodin

This book is dedicated in loving memory of Joanie Dugger. Joanie, through her steadfast dedication and service to Upper Arlington Schools as executive director of the Upper Arlington Education Foundation, has made a deep and lasting positive impact on our community.

www.mascotbooks.com

Golden Bears A to Z

For more information, please contact:
Mascot Books
620 Herndon Parkway, Suite 320
Herndon, VA 20170
info@mascotbooks.com

Library of Congress Control Number: 2019900365

CPSIA Code: PRT0519A
ISBN-13: 978-1-64307-246-3

Printed in the United States

Greensview Students and Staff
Illustrated by Jana Holland

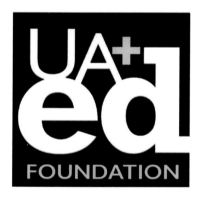

This project was graciously funded through a grant provided by the Upper Arlington Education Foundation and 100% of the proceeds go directly to support future grants.

A is for Arlington,
Where the Golden Bears roam.
A great place to live,
It's the town we call home.

Ohio

Arlington →

→ Upper Arlington

Arlington
Marble Cliff

In 1913 Ben and King Thompson purchased 840 acres of land from James T. Miller. The Thompsons wanted to name this new development Upper Arlington because it sat just north of an established area already called Arlington. However, there was another Arlington near Findlay, Ohio! The post office wanted to end the confusion; therefore, the Arlington near Findlay, Ohio kept its name, the other Arlington changed its name to Marble Cliff, and the Thompsons' land remained Upper Arlington.

B is for the buildings,
Built strong to last.
On the historic register,
They give us a glimpse into the past.

The Upper Arlington Historic District, also known as Old Arlington, was placed on the National Register of Historic Places in 1985. Notable structures include Jones Middle School and Fire Station No. 71, which served as UA's first municipal building.

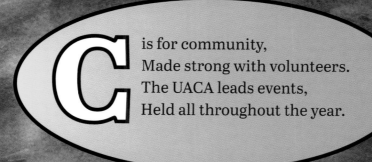

C is for community,
Made strong with volunteers.
The UACA leads events,
Held all throughout the year.

Since 1933, volunteers in the Upper Arlington Civic Association
(UACA) have organized and run community events that enrich the lives of
UA residents. Popular UACA events throughout the year include the Golden
Bear Scare, the Easter Candy Hunt, the 4th of July Parade, the Memorial
Day Run, and Christmas in the Park.

D is for the distinctions,
Our great town receives.
For accomplishments of alumni,
And even for our trees.

The Upper Arlington Alumni Association recognizes many notable citizens through the Outstanding Alumnus Award and the Distinguished Alumnus Award. Honorees include Nobel Prize winner Dr. George Smoot (Class of 1962) and actress Beverly D'Angelo (Class of 1969).

Upper Arlington is designated as a Tree City USA and has over 17,000 street trees and thousands of other trees throughout the community, many of which are over 100 years old.

E is for education,
A point of pride here in UA.
With teachers like Mary Boyer,
Our schools have grown along the way.

Mary Boyer, as one of the first teachers in the community, taught 13 students in the basement of King Thompson's home from 1917 to 1918.

Currently Upper Arlington is home to Upper Arlington High School, Jones and Hastings Middle Schools, and five elementary schools: Barrington, Greensview, Tremont, Wickliffe, and Windermere, as well as Burbank Early Childhood School. Other schools located in UA include The Wellington School, Saint Agatha, and St. Andrew School.

F is for families,
Residents both young and old.
UA is home to citizens,
Who are loyal to the black and gold.

Upper Arlington is home to roughly 35,000 residents. UA's sense of community, events, and schools make it a great place for all to live. Many people who are born and raised in Upper Arlington return to the community to raise their own families.

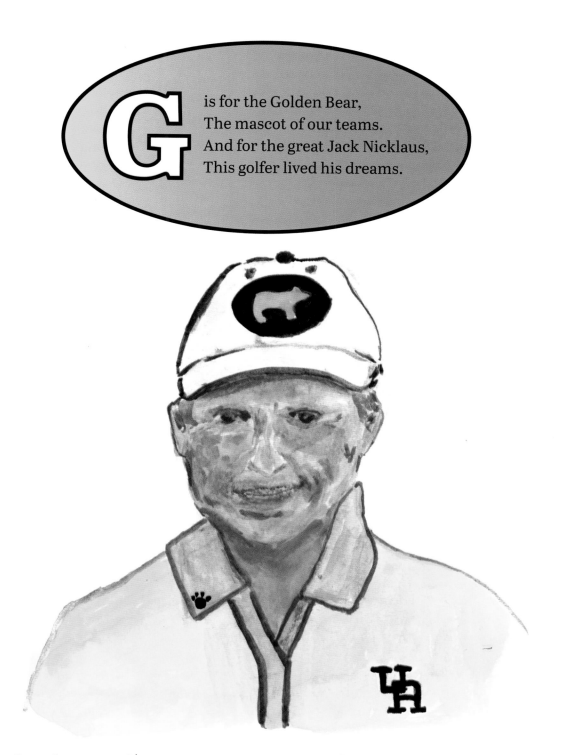

The Golden Bear became UA's mascot in 1928. Known as "The Golden Bear," golfer Jack Nicklaus was born and raised in UA and graduated from Upper Arlington High School in 1957. Nicklaus had one of the greatest professional golf careers in history.

H is for heroes,
Veterans honored for their strength.
And for police and firefighters,
Who protect us at great length.

Police, firefighters, and veterans have a respected history of keeping our country, state, and city safe. The Upper Arlington Police and Fire Departments have served our community since the 1920s. Veterans are honored with a memorial called Veterans Plaza located at Mallway Park near Jones Middle School.

I is for the Ice House,
Found on the Miller Farm.
The house still stands today,
With its history and charm.

The Miller Ice House, located on the grounds of First Community Village, was built in 1860 and used by the Miller family for many years to store ice cut from the Scioto River. In the summers, the Miller sisters would host lemonade parties at the ice house. This historic building is still open to the community.

J is for July 4th,
Red, white, and blue all around.
With colorful fireworks and block parties,
And a parade that flows through town.

Upper Arlington began celebrating the 4th of July in the mid-1920s. Festivities begin with a parade down Northwest Boulevard. During the day, many families and neighbors gather for block parties and cookouts, followed by a colorful display of fireworks at Northam Park.

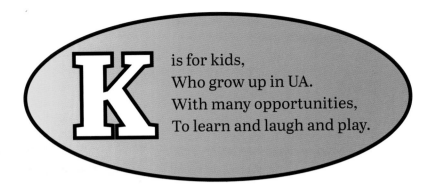

K is for kids,
Who grow up in UA.
With many opportunities,
To learn and laugh and play.

The Upper Arlington Parks and Recreation Department creates many opportunities for children and families throughout the year, including the Winter Festival, Spring Fling, Summer Celebration, and Fall Fest.

UA is also home to several kid-focused businesses including Picassos art studio and Cover to Cover children's bookstore.

L is for libraries,
Storytime and books to read.
Miller Park, Main, and Lane,
Fun for all, guaranteed!

Public libraries are a valued part of the Upper Arlington
community. Miller Park Library, UA's first library, was
established in 1942. Prior to that, the building served as
a shelter for streetcar passengers, as well as a voting
location. The Main Library was established in 1959 followed
by the Lane Road branch in 1975.

M is for the marching band,
Music and the arts.
The song, "Dear Old Arlington,"
Lives on in all our hearts.

The Upper Arlington Marching Band began in 1929 with 36 members, and has since performed at professional football games, college bowl games, and even a Disney festival.

The City of Upper Arlington and its schools have strong cultural and performing arts programs featuring plays and exhibits throughout the year.

N is for Norwester,
UA's first newspaper.
It's now the high school yearbook,
A big community shaper.

The Norwester magazine was published from 1917 to 1922 and reported on life in Upper Arlington, Grandview Heights, and Marble Cliff. Since 1923, the Norwester has served as the Upper Arlington High School yearbook.

O is for Ohio,
Our state's the heart of it all.
With UA in the middle,
We all stand proud and tall.

In 1803 Ohio became the 17th state admitted to the Union. Columbus is the state capital and largest city in Ohio, of which Upper Arlington is a suburb.

P is for the parks and pools,
Great places to hang out and play.
Biking, walking, swimming, and sports,
There's enough to fill your day.

Upper Arlington is home to 21 parks and three community pools. In 2018, as part of the centennial celebration, a life-size bronze sculpture of a mother "Golden Bear" and her two cubs was added to Centennial Plaza in Northam Park.

Q is for the quarry,
One of the largest in the land.
Its limestone rock was used,
To make buildings that still stand.

From the mid-1800s to the 1980s, the Marble Cliff Quarry Company in Upper Arlington operated the largest limestone quarry in the United States. The quarry stretched from the Scioto River to the Olentangy River.

Stone from the quarry was used to help build the LeVeque Tower, Ohio Stadium, and the Ohio Statehouse. Today, the quarry is being redeveloped into a park.

R is for restaurants,
Local places to talk and eat.
Burgers, pizzas, even cinnamon sticks,
There are plenty of tasty treats.

Tremont
Chef-O-Nette

Many great restaurants are staples in the Upper Arlington community, including Chef-O-Nette, Tommy's Pizza, Colin's Coffee, and Caffé DaVinci.

UA alumni and restaurateurs Cameron Mitchell (Cameron Mitchell Restaurants) and Jeni Britton Bauer (Jeni's Splendid Ice Creams) are well-known both in and outside of the community.

S is for shops,
Tremont, Kingsdale, the
Mallway, and more.
The local businesses we love,
Serve as UA's shopping core.

Stores in the Mallway began opening their doors in 1925. Several decades later the Lane Avenue Shopping Center opened in 1949 and became the largest shopping center in the city at that time. That same year, Kingsdale Shopping Center opened, and original tenant Argo & Lehne Jewelers remains in business today. Tremont Center opened in 1951 and is still home to several original stores including Huffman's Market and The Original Goodie Shop.

T is for traditions,
Labor Day is one of the best.
With bike races and the festival,
This day rises above the rest!

The Labor Day Arts Festival began as a small event put together by neighbors. In 1966 it was held at Miller Park, but as it grew, the festival moved to the municipal services center and then Northam Park, where it remains today.

Other annual events held in Upper Arlington include the Golden Bear Bash hosted by the Upper Arlington Education Foundation as well as the 4th of July parade and fireworks.

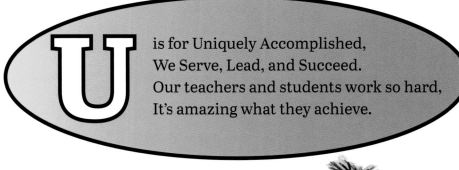

U is for Uniquely Accomplished,
We Serve, Lead, and Succeed.
Our teachers and students work so hard,
It's amazing what they achieve.

Upper Arlington schools are a point of pride in the community. Students in kindergarten through 12th grade focus on academics, but also participate in valuable service learning projects. The Upper Arlington Education Foundation provides funds for resources and programs to enhance student learning. Upper Arlington High School ranks among the best in the state of Ohio, and offers over 50 different clubs as well as the International Baccalaureate program.

Upper Arlington has a long history of excellence in athletics. With over 30 varsity sports, it's no wonder Upper Arlington High School teams have claimed over 140 state championships since 1930.

V is for victory,
The times our teams have won it all!
From football to swimming and water polo,
Lacrosse, tennis, and baseball.

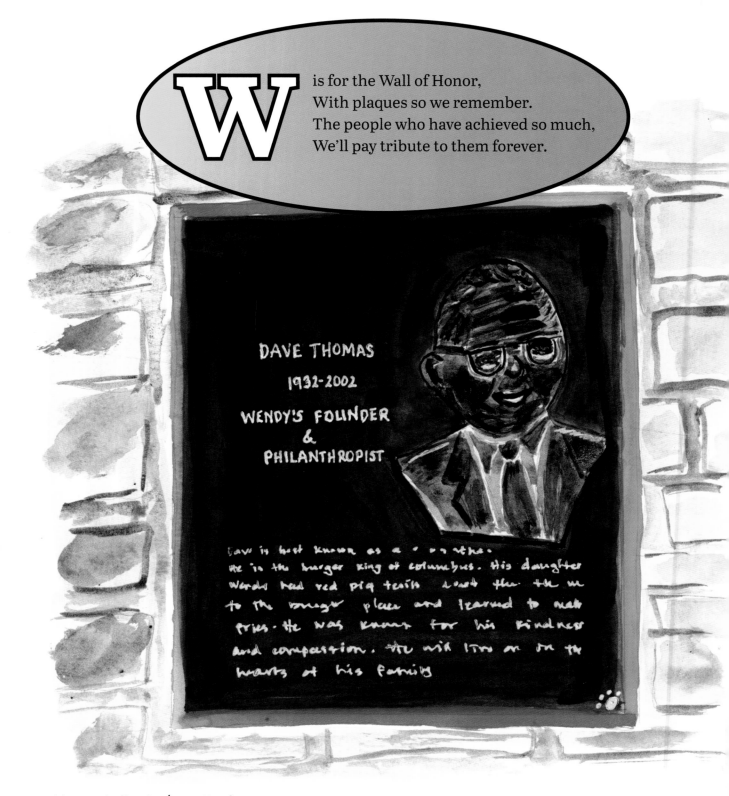

W is for the Wall of Honor,
With plaques so we remember.
The people who have achieved so much,
We'll pay tribute to them forever.

DAVE THOMAS
1932-2002

WENDY'S FOUNDER
&
PHILANTHROPIST

Upper Arlington's Wall of Honor recognizes citizens who have achieved greatness. Recipients include Wayne Woodrow (Woody) Hayes, Arthur G. James, M.D., Governor James A. Rhodes, L. Marv Moorehead, John W. Galbreath, Howard Dwight Smith, Stefanie Spielman, and Dave Thomas.

UA alumnus and Olympian Abby Johnston (2008 graduate) won a silver medal for synchronized diving at the 2012 Summer Olympic Games in London. She finished 12th at the 2016 Olympic Games in Rio in the individual 3 meter diving event.

Blake Haxton (2009 graduate) served as a member of the Upper Arlington High School crew team. In his graduating year, Blake lost his legs to a rare bacterial infection. However, this did not stop him from rowing! He finished 4th place at the 2016 International Paralympic Games in an individual rowing event.

X is for eXcellence,
Olympic dreams were born here.
Alumni like Haxton and Johnston,
Have shown determination without fear.

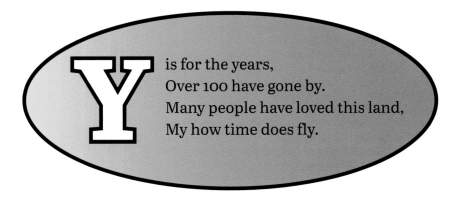

Y is for the years,
Over 100 have gone by.
Many people have loved this land,
My how time does fly.

Notable people have contributed to what is now "our UA." Freed slave and master blacksmith, Pleasant Litchford, who was the 4th largest landowner in the area at the time, previously owned land that is now part of Upper Arlington.

Many landmarks and traditions have stood the test of time throughout Upper Arlington's history. The city of Upper Arlington's centennial year was celebrated in 2018.

Z is for zooming,
Together year after year.
Our future is golden,
Let's give UA a cheer!

Many changes are leading Upper Arlington into its next 100 years. With new schools, parks, building developments, and the wonderful people found here, Upper Arlington's future looks bright!

Way to go,
You've finished the book.
Here's a list of places to visit,
Go out and take a look.

Amelita Mirolo Barn

Argo & Lehne Jewelers

Barrington Elementary School

Burbank Early Childhood School

Caffé DaVinci

Cameron Mitchell Restaurants

Centennial Plaza

Chef-O-Nette

Colin's Coffee

Cover to Cover Books for Young Readers

Devon Pool

Fire Station No. 71 & 72

Golden Bear mascot located in Upper Arlington High School

Greensview Elementary School

Hastings Middle School

Huffman's Market

Jeni's Splendid Ice Creams

Jones Middle School

Kingsdale Shopping Center

Lane Road Library

LeVeque Tower

Main Library

Mallway Park

Marv Moorehead Stadium

Miller Ice House

Miller Park

Miller Park Library

Moretti's

Northam Park

Ohio Stadium

Ohio State House

The Original Goodie Shop

Parade Route on Northwest Blvd

Picassos Art Studio

Quarry Trails Metro Park

Reed Road Water Park

Saint Agatha School

Saint Andrew School

Sunny 95 Park

Thompson Park

Tommy's Pizza

Tremont Elementary School

Tremont Pool

Tremont Shopping Center

Trophy Case at UAHS

UA Police Station in the Municipal Building

Upper Arlington High School

Veterans Plaza at Mallway Park

Wall of Honor at the Municipal Building

The Wellington School

Wickliffe Progressive School

Windermere Elementary School